THE BACK HOME SERIES

SERIES TITLES

In the Room at the Top of the World

Cheering for a sports team—I mean, seriously cheering—for a sports team requires unwavering faith, enthusiasm, and, at times, an ability to suffer. But the reward is greater than ephemeral entertainment. Being a good fan means becoming part of a shared history, a shared narrative. *In the Room at the Top of the World* is Ben McCormick's heartfelt, lyrical account of a year of magical thinking. This is a book that calls into question what it means to belong; to a region (my beloved Midwest), to a city (Milwaukee—my favorite misunderstood and overshadowed American metropolis), a family, and a team (in this case, the World Champion Milwaukee Bucks). This is a book about a man learning to accept himself and the flawed world around him and it reads like a Giannis Antetokounmpo fast break slam dunk—you'll race right through it and hope that McCormick has another project publishing sooner rather than later.

—NICKOLAS BUTLER
author of *Shotgun Lovesongs* and *A Forty Year Kiss*

Ben does a beautiful job showing how something as simple as sports can bring you closer to home even when you're half a country away. *In the Room at the Top of the World* finds the humor, joy, and grit of the Midwest, but the soul of the book will hit any heart away from home.

—CHARLIE BERENS
comedian & *New York Times* Bestselling Author
creator of the *Manitowoc Minute*

As he chronicles the Bucks' 23 postseason games, Ben McCormick brilliantly captures Milwaukee's complicated existence as a segregated and nationally-panned city that vacillates between local pride and Midwestern humility, while also illustrating sports' inherent ability to foster identity and connection—even from afar. Even if McCormick's experiences in the summer of '21 don't mirror yours, they're compelling, and they helped stir up my memories—from watching "The Valley Oop" in a crowded bar to processing Giannis' devastating injury and immaculate recovery to seeing post-pandemic Milwaukee coming together to celebrate our long-awaited moment in the sun—when the city was at the center of the sports universe.

—TYLER MAAS
co-founder and editor of *Milwaukee Record*

What does it mean to root for the home team? It's a question central to the culture of sports, and *In the Room at the Top of World*, Ben McCormick takes a deep dive into both his own life and the fortunes of the Milwaukee Bucks during their 2020-21 season to provide answers. In the process, he demonstrates how deep and complex the subject can be. Readers are sure to be dazzled by the leaps and connections McCormick makes as he moves from sport to personal identity to ideas of home.

—LARRY WATSON
author of *The Lives of Edie Pritchard*

In the Room at the Top of the World

Leaving the Midwest, the Bucks Title Run, and Other Survivals

Ben McCormick

CORNERSTONE PRESS
UNIVERSITY OF WISCONSIN-STEVENS POINT

Cornerstone Press, Stevens Point, Wisconsin 54481
Copyright © 2025 Ben McCormick
Illustrations © 2025 Allen Parker II
www.uwsp.edu/cornerstone

Printed in the United States of America.

Library of Congress Control Number: 2025943466
ISBN: 978-1-968148-05-8

Cornerstone Press titles are produced in courses and internships offered by the Department of English at the University of Wisconsin–Stevens Point.

DIRECTOR & PUBLISHER
Dr. Ross K. Tangedal

EXECUTIVE EDITORS
Jeff Snowbarger, Freesia McKee

EDITORIAL DIRECTOR
Brett Hill

SENIOR EDITORS
Paige Biever, Eva Nielsen, Reilly Crous

PRESS STAFF
Jacob Childress, Alex Diaz, Lilly Kulbeck, Sam Zajkowski, Allison Lange, Sophie McPherson, Sam Bjork, Madison Schultz, Autumn Vine

To My Family

CONTENTS

Conference Finals: Atlanta Hawks

NBA Finals: Phoenix Suns

I love Milwaukee… It's a very special part of America that's full of promise but also full of pain.

—Matthew Desmond, *Evicted*

I think God would want us to go to Milwaukee.

—Michael Kelso, *That '70s Show*

First Round:

Miami Heat

Khris Middleton Faded Back

20.7 SECONDS REMAINING: GORAN DRAGIC turned a Jimmy Butler airball into a corner three to tie the game, and I started bargaining with whatever available god would still extend my credit line. From my futon I promised not to celebrate a victory—no—I'd just sigh relief. This is what upper midwesterners do: we barter away our own joy. If we won I'd just say "thank you." That was how early 2021 had gone—that January, in a Texas college town I was desperate to leave, I made myself that empty promise: this would be my year.

But that's not what we do. Khris Middleton faded back, and he could never have sprung from Milwaukee's central vein of a river. Think about our favorite sons and daughters: Gene Wilder? His mother shipped him off to real art school at fifteen when we couldn't support his radiance. Oprah? High school at Nicolet and gone. Anyone from here who's done anything great left to do it somewhere bigger. There's an inertia that seems to drive the destined, and I was high enough on my own youthful promise to mistake my restlessness for something else.

I'd arrived south of Austin, Texas with a fellowship at college to teach and write my great novel, and by the time the Bucks made the 2021 playoffs three years later I'd arrived in Portland, Oregon, with no book deal and a few burned bridges. In those years I'd dropped fifty pounds to be toned and desirable and then gained it all back. I told a woman I'd always love her and then stopped. I'd been absolutely convinced I'd become a bestselling writer and been wrong, then convinced I'd teach literature the rest of my life for the children (the children!) and been wrong—Gene Wilder, Tony Shalhoub, or Liberace I was not. Just as annoying: I didn't feel any wiser than I did before when I was full of positive affirmations about how *of course* I would write an international bestseller. This is the place a darkness that has periodically threatened my place on Earth takes hold: if I couldn't make good on their belief, then maybe they never knew the real me and it might be best if no one did. Once, just once, I wanted to be all the way right about myself. As it happened, I was also three years into watching almost every Bucks game. Giannis Antetokounmpo fostered a rare agreement between my mind and body: I should really sit and watch this. What I still can't explain is how I'm so certain I was more than bearing witness to him. I participated. Maybe this is sports fandom as refuge: when I can no longer give over to myself, it's something to believe in.

The week before this game we'd been taking shrapnel from all sides: a full week of national media calling Heat Culture the favorite despite the Bucks being the seeding favorite. What were the Milwaukee Bucks but a small market side quest on the Heat's odyssey anyway? When a more important part of the country that appears on cable TV or has a clothing line tells us who we are, at some point I think it's human to believe it. It took me four quarters plus a few minutes. But Khris Middleton isn't from Wisconsin. Khris came from South Carolina and worked through Texas before heading north. He didn't have practice taking himself apart.

What I'm saying about Milwaukee and its basketball team is sometimes good luck can break down your door, but in May 2021 it was already reading a magazine in our living room. The whole second half into overtime my brain wired my jaw shut. In a newer, larger apartment in Portland, I sat on a futon and shut the door so my partner who loved me wouldn't have to hear. We lived two-thousand-and-fifty-eight miles west of Milwaukee's western border, and if I shut myself off from the world I could collapse the distance without having to admit who I'd become. My first niece had just been born in Milwaukee, and I was the only family member yet to meet her. Nothing of mine hung on the walls. All I had was my cheesehead coaster on the coffee table and the TV.

But then Khris Middleton faded back. He faded away from Duncan Robinson in overtime. And there's a moment when the ball leaves his fingertips that's special to the last seconds of any game. Where everyone—including the players—stops. Basketball is the only major American sport where after the shot leaves the hand, it's on God. An opponent can't rob it from the air or dive to save the shot—the die has been cast. In the air hangs chance itself. Belief. It isn't stars aligning if it goes in. It's angles. Cuts. Form. Breath. Your year, just this once. And once again an ember flickered in a place people left so they might kindle a flame.

Like many of you, my friends, I wasn't raised to ask for more than was lovingly spooned onto my plate, and so I am tempted to be grateful for a win or a good bounce when it comes. It is not in many of our natures to be demanding centers of gravity the way New York or LA might, but we are marked by what we excuse. This song is for Khris Middleton who left home to make another. This song is for taking up space at the right time. This song is for years that have passed and moments I have missed; joys I starved myself of because just when I think I'm out, a place tries to pull me back in, and I either love myself or hate myself enough to stay away. This song is for bloodies with beer chasers, for bubblers, and for Gene fucking Wilder.

I have imagined my obituary, and people will not gloss over its first sentence: "Ben McCormick came of age at home, and he died thinking about it too: Milwaukee, Wisconsin."

Trevor Ariza Turned Old and He Never Saw It Coming

WHEN YOU GIVE UP SEVENTY-EIGHT POINTS in a half, it isn't just not your night—it belongs to somebody else. Trevor Ariza was in his tenth year of trying to recapture magic from winning a title with Kobe Bryant in 2009 which turned him into a millionaire many times over. GMs spoke of him as a championship player, one of the first true 3 and D wings teams needed for a deep playoff run. But the Heat were his ninth team in ten years. He'd traveled hundreds of thousands of miles, dedicated himself to the gym and a ten-foot hoop every day, and he hadn't won a thing since. How clean are memories after ten years? How many stay at all?

They called him a Giannis stopper. It's a job title assigned to wings or bigs who are usually 6'8 or taller, weigh 215+, and can move their feet well enough to take a charge. Every team has a Giannis stopper which is funny in how the phrase itself is a fantasy. I suppose it is raw confidence that separates elite athletes from the rest of us. Brian Scalabrine, who never held a starting NBA role in his career, famously said, "I am closer to LeBron than you are to me." And that night the Heat were down twenty-five when Ariza bricked a three, and Giannis beat him out in transition. Ariza sprinted hard. But there is a swift grace about the way Giannis runs the floor that Ariza couldn't match. So when Giannis went up for a thunderous dunk to make it a twenty-seven-point lead, Ariza bearhugged him, twisted, and drove a shoulder into Giannis's chest. Ariza executed a full-form NFL tackle. That night, he gave up on basketball's rules, the fairness that had been so kind to him all his career, and the warm promise of ever winning another title. He'd play one more sunset season in LA for the league minimum, but in many ways his career ended two minutes into the third quarter on a humid Monday night in Milwaukee.

I lost respect for him being unable to handle a drubbing, but I also pity a thirty-seven year-old giving his all to keep a young man from galloping for an easy two when that young man wasn't even playing basketball when Ariza first stepped on an NBA floor. The game that had given a man the greatest success in his life, generational wealth, and purpose had passed him by, but it hadn't happened just then. It had likely happened weeks, months, even years earlier. Trevor Ariza wondered stride-by-stride—Giannis's in-and-out steps springing into a dance—how the world could have changed so much these few years despite having his eyes open the whole time. This was his life now: fighting to keep twenty-five points down from becoming twenty-seven.

Ariza laid on top of Giannis and stayed there. They had a moment, or more accurately: Ariza stole one. Go back and watch the tape. The jerseys nearly fall away. The façade of sport drops, and Trevor Ariza doesn't belong anymore. Everyone moved toward the free throw line, but Ariza stayed on top of Giannis. He took back the only thing he could from a game that had already taken everything from him: he exerted the only power left over the man who had already beaten him.

He pressed Giannis's chest and thigh to raise himself to his feet. Yes—he pressed a jersey, but after the whistle it's only a person. Table scraps of a career. Put another way: it was the last thing he could cling to. In that moment Trevor Ariza needed Giannis to be alive in any of the ways he'd told himself for over the last decade. A lifeline. The only way to succeed on a basketball floor is to make the other nine players feel your gravity. Basketball had passed him by. If he didn't feel Giannis—if Giannis didn't feel *him*—he was gone.

Let me tell you what being a sports fan is: intimacy.

It's a removal of boundary—exposure. It's skin, then muscle, then tissue and tendons that stretch over bones. It's as intimate as the nerves exposed to the human pressure we are always gambling will be warm and not the heat of writhing pain. It isn't hedging—it is full bore without exception or excuse. Uncut. And so I am asking you to believe me saying that when Trevor Ariza pressed Giannis's chest and thigh that I felt it. And from the TV room in Portland, I suppose that I was once again in a new city trying to reinvent myself as the ideal Ben while doing so in a room with a closed door. I was reaching whatever version of myself existed without anyone watching. Like Clark Kent leaving a phone booth but in reverse.

The chest is a place of strength and the thigh a site of delicacy, so when someone's palms touch them both it is a flashbulb of complete control. It's that vulnerable cloud where an act can either be love, a transgression, or both. And the maleness of sports fandom is training wheels for life's vulnerable moments we either loathe to or are unprepared to feel—for sports are something we can take seriously at face value. What else can we call allowing oneself to be devoured by a twenty-four second possession or an online trade machine but "love?" It's puppy love: that sugary kind. It is a curious thing that I fight a hitch in my voice to tell my mother I love her but not when I say, "I love the Bucks." It's only a shame until you accept that fandom is a warm bed and a good meal for parts of us kept behind a closed door that we desperately need to keep alive. It's hope. And the magic is when we share that vulnerability to joy and pain in an arena or a group chat we see ourselves in the world and the world in us.

It is mostly a pleasing feeling to be less alone.

I know many writers who have written on the vitality of finding "your people," and I am enough of an ambitious attention hog to have avoided this subset of my people for nearly thirty years: basketball nerds.

WHEN I WAS EIGHTEEN, I set my motorcycle helmet on a musician friend's kitchen island. We'd been tight for years but I was fashioning myself a real artist so I wanted to spend more time with his guitars and his family's prowess, then all five came in one-by-one and asked who it belonged to, aghast each time at the possibility it could belong to me. One of his brothers accused me of some kind of unfunny prank—I just didn't fit the profile. But they weren't jerks; they were right. Sometimes you look around, and your people aren't really your people at all, and that's one of my constant fears: turning out like Trevor Ariza again and again in this life. That the person I want to be is so far gone I'll lose the handhold on a cliff. And

I'll have my cheap moment of power before realizing what everyone else saw first: Giannis had actually thrown the ball toward the hoop. And it had bounced in. Twenty-five wasn't becoming twenty-seven—it actually became twenty-eight.

In my TV room, I tried not to make too much noise but a warmth bloomed inside me knowing Miami was hurting. This is the other thing about intimacy: honesty. I am told by myself that I do not want people to hurt, but in the TV room I could admit I wanted them to. I fear today what that says about me. That if I had to define myself or my city by where Miami was in proximity to me, I wanted them under my palms. I wanted them to know I was there. And I do not know how to tell the difference between when to accept yourself and when to sell your gear and try something else, but watching Trevor Ariza experience the moment he overstayed his welcome in the NBA made me feel a little less alone.

The Place with the Best Hash Browns in Town Has Swastikas in the Floor

"BUT THEY'RE FACING THE OTHER WAY," multiple Milwaukeeans tell me who may be surprised to learn they're pro-swastika. They're painted into the occasional tile and the size of a silver dollar. Twenty-one in total if you're counting.

The diner's space is a pre-neon, pre-Elvis time capsule—remarkably open. A large man worked the griddle behind the counter, opened his palms and asked what I'll have then kept it all in his head. Fresh blueberries in their syrup toppled onto lemon poppyseed pancakes. But the hash browns. My fork snapped through the neat rectangle's surface and glided through the butter goodness beneath. I try not to look down.

Milwaukee's history can be felt in your feet. Anyone in Milwaukee knows where they're welcome by its firm boundaries—if you're white: east of I-43 and north of I-94. If you're not, come on in if you're spending money or stay home. I've been warned by people looking out for me to stay north of the Menominee Valley that cuts across the city's waist.

We were once two separate cities on either side of the Milwaukee River out of spite. Solomon Juneau and Byron Kilbourn misaligned their streets and started up a war where citizens built bridges and burned them in the same day for weeks on end. This is why Milwaukee's bridges are now and have always been at odd angles—concrete dropping out to holey grates on a bridge and picking you back up in a new place. You know if you're welcome in that part of the city by how the ground greets your feet or registers an anxious lightness that it might mean it's time to head home. In a city so segregated it helped Matthew Desmond win a Pulitzer, the ground speaks clearly.

I could stop eating the best hash browns in town on a principle—my love can stretch itself taut that way. But it's not a "could" as much as a "should" that never happened. Because if I started truly living what I call my values, I don't know how many memories of Milwaukee I'd get to replay when I'm back home to visit. We live on stolen land and borrowed time. But every time I'm home I check those tiles to see if someone's etched them out or painted them over—the smallest improvement. But they're still there. And I sit down anyway. The more that years go by and memories melt away, the more I hold on to whatever I can from Milwaukee—even its worst parts. I think it's easy to get rosy about something or someplace once you leave it, but I'd like to hold the whole thing. I want to love the city that made me in that bell hooks way—complete honesty. I want to love Milwaukee and demand in that love and be tender in that love and love myself in that love. It's burning coals and embers in the back of my brain, and it's easy to love the warmth. It's something else to love the sear.

I HAVE BEEN HAVING A DREAM where I am driving a car and it hydroplanes. The steering wheel turns light and playful. Back and forth it goes. The tire rubber and pavement are so slick they're silent. I grapple for control that never comes—turn the wheel and turn it again. My skin prickles waiting to be crushed. Until finally the car stops. The steering wheel is tough and disagreeable again, but the prickle remains. Here's something Milwaukeeans believe about driving in the rain or snow: the real danger is the other drivers. I am stopped but I don't look in the rearview mirror. I could see who might be charging forward ready to collapse my sternum into the carburetor, but I never do.

How I think about that has changed over the last couple years, but I think now it's got at least something to do with the dregs of Catholicism I can't quite shake from the first eighteen years of my life. I might think of myself as non-religious, but there's a foundation in me it wove itself into. World-pulling things don't happen in cities like Milwaukee, and when I wonder why I believe something out there is pulling on a string. We're still paying for sins, and as long as we keep making them we always will. It's some kind of equilibrium we never stray too far from. And what I'm finding out right now is it might even be a reason I can move away from Milwaukee but can never get it out of my head. It's a reason I love it: that particular kind of Catholic, all-over sting of shame. Because God is always watching, and it is easier for me to feel at home in shame and just desserts than it is to accept the randomness of the universe.

THE HEAT ARE NOT BORED but worn. If Kendrick Nunn or Goran Dragic want a clean look at the rim they have to fight Jrue Holiday to a screen, body up Brook Lopez, and round the lane for a fadeaway. In the second quarter, Miami were so desperate to reverse this avalanche they went to a zone. It didn't work. Heat fans themselves turned into a better golf audience than a basketball one, and somehow I still couldn't shake the thought that the Bucks might fuck this up. I might've been the first to believe they could win the title but was the last to believe they could win a single game. The best sins are the ones we pay for right away. Others wait for their right day. They might wait a long time.

Post-game, Mike Budenholzer says, "Our focus, our attention to detail, has got to stay high." But in a game where you pursue something, what does it mean to ask yourself to stay yourself when that hasn't won a championship in fifty years?

In 1975, four years after winning Milwaukee its first NBA title, Kareem Abdul-Jabbar demanded a trade due to "cultural differences" with Milwaukee. He said, "I don't have any family or friends here. The things I relate to don't happen to be in this city to any meaningful degree. Culturally, what I'm about and what Milwaukee is about are two different things." It doesn't take a genius to know what a Black, Muslim superstar meant by this, and it also doesn't take a genius to understand. We have much practice in greatness leaving our city, and either you're a chosen people or you have to put in the work. And change moves at the rate of tectonic plates before they scrape and level a skyline.

Up 3-0, I could've looked in that rearview mirror to see what was coming, but I didn't. I just wanted to feel under my feet, let myself believe that whatever was coming wouldn't be an end. That I might be alive for a moment when Milwaukee left the cosmic red. That something had begun.

Fuck a Gentleman

AND THEIR SWEEP. LET THEM WIN ONE TO look classy, my ass. And while you're at it, do not mess with Jrue Holiday's bag, and do not mess with Brook Lopez period.

Please excuse me for having had an extra bottle of High Life that night. Check that—I'm not asking; I'm telling. The Miami Heat were Bubble Frauds.

Giannis preached table manners about not playing with your food, but I was thinking most about two players who found ways to sneak their elbows onto the table and pick scraps from their teeth. You will say the names Jrue Holiday and Brook Lopez, and you will do so with respect. It's everything you see and more you don't—I'm talking about footwork featured in Coach Bud's First Symphony: "Play Random." Jrue's hesi is the long sweep of a bow across a cello and his crossover a lightning strike staccato. Brook might seem to lumber through the lane but it is the low, rhythmic thump of a bass drum.

The Miami Heat were Bubble Frauds. I was being a little loose and loud that night because I was trying to be a little loose and loud. There was a novel unfamiliarity to it I don't care for in hindsight. I'd have liked to have yelled down my residential avenue of Portland houses and little wooden libraries while I had a right to it. But on that breezy evening I couldn't let go that some of Milwaukee's reputation is its truth: a welcoming place; not a fortress. We are not a people who—once we've pinned our opponent to the mat—kill. I don't think I'm the only one of us who before that night almost preferred to give the Heat just one win so the postseries handshakes and hugs would come gracious and kind. We're a type of people who during the fourth game wouldn't have mentioned the sweep out loud—my people take jinxes and humility seriously. Our outward joy is a fleeting thing which makes it a precious thing—as backwards as it sounds we take pride in looking humble. I know this because I live this particular contradiction. But that night we tasted honey made from what felt like destiny. These Bucks reside in Milwaukee but have come from everywhere else—they saw 3-0 and said, "trust us: this is the promised land."

We used to apologize for you: it's okay you didn't know Milwaukee was actually great. How we'll hold the door open for a stranger quite a way from the door and wish them good morning, or how Lake Michigan gleams in the morning, or how frozen custard is better than ice cream. Before that night, we'd have just been thankful you knew at all. But this was the game we believed. From then on, my people looked inward and liked what we saw so much that our conscience slammed the brakes but our mouths ran on—shame on you for not knowing. Miami is over. Intoxication is our thing; tomorrow be damned.

Put some respect on Jrue Holiday and Brook Lopez's names. How dare you be late to this party, and how sweet it is to be here. The Miami Heat were Bubble Frauds. And ten thousand in Milwaukee's Deer District screamed for a team playing a full time zone away and discovered the size of true themselves by the size of the echo that came back to them. By how when raindrops started to fall they felt as if they could summon the woodwinds and the brass and the strings and play them right back into the sky.

IN PORTLAND THAT NIGHT, the rain fell light and constant. Looking at the first pictures and videos from the Deer District, Milwaukee's new city center, made Milwaukee a discernibly different place than I had ever known. But I chose to believe it hadn't changed at all. This is the dissonant wonder of leaving home that isn't unlike a distant crush: I could invent whatever version of Milwaukee I liked without repercussion—a fantasy that no one's around to disprove is real enough to feel true. It's even easier to do when the beer flows and the team wins, and I'm trying not to begrudge myself moments of joy as much these days. What a night that was, something wholly new while the picture frames holding my parents, brothers, friends, and myself grew brittle in still-unpacked boxes. Their glass chips a little more all the time. Fogs. The Bucks helped me build a glass prison of my own choosing—I wasn't in Milwaukee anymore, but the magic of sport made me feel as if the rickety house of my identity and its geography was still up to code. And I must be honest—I love that prison. That fiction I could be in two places at once. That I could have it all: judge my relic of a hometown from my new life without having to break myself open.

Conference Semifinals:

Brooklyn Nets

I Met My Niece Kaylee the Night She Was Born and She Is Already Older

I WOULDN'T DISCOVER THE COLOR OF HER
eyes until a different FaceTime days later. But I didn't

begrudge her sleep. One month before Brooklyn game one, it seemed like a rather traumatizing day all around.

My brother and sister-in-law looked bewildered in that new parent way when "going through the motions" is also aspirational. It was as though they'd found a football, swaddled the thing, and were playacting parenthood in exaggerated lullabies and whispers for a kid that was already asleep. My mother wore her iPhone like a lanyard, and while I was with my family in that moment, I wouldn't say I was sharing in it. What I could do was ask questions like I always do on the phone because conversation is currency when you're this far away. We've never been a family who can just sit in silence. There is either a thing to do or a thing about to be done or we head home. We are "wired this way"—a family where the TV is always on and it fills the gaps.

That night I was the TV. I was a rerun without anything to say but trying to be involved. Instead, I witnessed. I witnessed my mother become a grandmother. I witnessed my father become a grandfather. I witnessed the founding of a new generation—a concrete foundation laid that made my family feel grandiose in its history and promise. We all, somehow, become our parents. That night was a coronation of four adults pressing through one of life's one-way doors at the hands of a sleeping child. And I stayed the same.

The day of game one, Kaylee's eyes were blue. I'd bought her a Giannis onesie far too big for her and my brother dutifully wrapped her in it anyway. When we FaceTimed, she seemed obsessed with me but really it was her weeks-old brain gluing itself to the psychedelic wonder of the smartphone. I had never really met this child, but I was struck at the power of my desire to walk her around my neighborhood in Portland. I pitched my brother on loading his one-month-old daughter and her new mother on connecting flights. I'd been away four years, and that was the first time I was sure I was missing out on something back home that I'd never get back. A scale had been pressed. It had a way of making every growler fill and waterfall hike in Portland trivial. I wanted to show Kaylee the hundred-foot-tall pines near my apartment and the parks I ran through. I wanted to push her on a swing. How amazing it is the way a new-born creates momentum and purpose from a stationary position. Desire from nothing—from *elsewhere*. I grew up through Catholic school like so many others in the Milwaukee area. When I saw her, it was the first time in years I felt closer to whoever God used to be to me.

The Bucks shot six for thirty from three, and I guess that's real faith: having no earthly idea if missing over and over again indicates something real—even having some evidence it is—and choosing to keep going anyway. Call it an underdog story, call it stupidity, but I'd somehow tied my sense of worth in the world and the worth of my home to whether a group of fifteen men surrounded by coaches and staff could slay a three-headed dragon: Kevin

Durant, James Harden, and Kyrie Irving. Sports had a stark clarity that I still can't find in much else. Where my niece was a wonderful question, a win or a loss was something I could hold, feel its aliveness in my palms. I think it's okay to need that. Pessimism usually catches me game one in a playoff series, but that night something felt different than fifty previous years of failures built on high seeds and self-doubts. I wouldn't have called myself confident, but I was doing my old religious thing where no matter what I see, a grain of belief sows itself in my gut and I choose to believe anyway. Desire from somewhere else. I thought I'd left behind the atomic power of seeing something true and instead vaporizing it. But the easy clarity of a win or a loss isn't what makes me come alive. It's that great and terrible thing: conviction.

Let Me Tell You a Secret

I WOULD'VE LIKED TO TALK SHIT ABOUT Blake Griffin but I couldn't. I would've liked to talk shit about a man who quit on his Detroit teammates acting like he couldn't dunk for a couple years and suddenly arrived on a new team rearing back like it's 2015 again. Or about how the only thing to call a person who premeditates hip checks and stepping over fallen opponents is a snake. But lately I had been trying to foreground myself. So when Griffin baseline cut to an open rim that begged him to bend it, I instead wrote about how Giannis was guarding him and over-helped as Giannis sometimes did. Or wrote about how PJ and Brook couldn't sew shut every passing window for Kevin Durant to hit Bruce Brown on the short roll. Or wrote about how Pat Connaughton couldn't slide to take Brown's path to the lane. And while we talk about life and game in the language of whether it was "good" or "bad," I cannot help noting that what I was choosing to foreground was not what I must've written about: that most days are right about medium and not the absolute pits like a thirty-nine-point loss to go down 2-0. But at some point, a trend becomes a reality and not a bad dream from which we shake ourselves awake.

Instead, I am telling secrets because it is time to tell a truth: I want to be in Portland.

It strikes me that who we are may be a matter of borders. Every person—especially ones from places that are only cable news fodder once every four years—necessarily define their self by what surrounds them. I could see where KD, Harden, Kyrie, and Blake ended on the floor, and it didn't make me feel good about what space that left me. It is not a far distance to wonder in what other ways I am delusional about myself and have just scratched the scales from my eyes to see. What if someone else is just better? Again. Like every other year.

"Beauty is in the eye of the beholder" is something adults used to say to me to make me feel better about being a pudgy, acne-laden kid. But to behold is to look at something or someone directly, and I still don't care to do it in the mirror. Even in reflection we never see the whole of ourselves—there's always an object of focus. For me: stomach, thighs, teeth. To look at myself directly is often a matter of assembling a mosaic from dozens of portholes of flaws. This is why I must write about what I don't want to admit, that the Bucks—that I—might've looked in the eyes of the people we loved and saw that we were not someone we respected. I would've liked to talk my shit about Blake Griffin—that I hope the IRS audited the piss out of him—but if we were to stand a chance at being great I must've looked at myself and asked the honest question I tell myself only does me harm: What if I'm not exceptional at all? That I did all this nonsense just to be another something in a long line of anonymous somethings? This is the bet that I have hedged in making a life somewhere else. It's a bet I have won. Here is the secret: some distant parts of me are eroding, devolving, metastasizing, and dying 2,058 miles away and I still want to be here. Try the beer a mile from where the hops are grown. Try a croissant where the freshwater lakes feed the yeast. Ski down Mount Hood and tell yourself Alpine Valley still makes your heart race the same way. RSVP to weddings "Regretfully Declines" because of the distance and shed the social obligation so you can be alone. Let me tell you the real secret: I like spending time with the person I am now more than I ever did the person I was in Wisconsin.

I have been trying to foreground myself and I want my family and friends of three years ago to spend time with this Me. But how quickly I know I'd atrophy. How eager and desperate for approval I'd be to reprise my role for people I can see in front of me but still pray are the person I remember. A half decade wasn't far enough yet in my late twenties. How quickly I'd throw whole years away to say, "it's 2015 again."

Rock Fight

I SUPPOSE THE METAPHOR HAS TO DO with the difficulty of the heft of a rock lifted toward a hoop, but if someone tells me a rock fight is about to break out I'm mostly concerned with keeping my skull intact. It is always a matter of safety in the playoffs, of how close you are to a perilous loss total. Scoring eighty-six points any other night would've landed the Bucks in that 3-0 Hellhole, but tonight it gave them one firm hand on a cliff's edge.

It is with the utmost respect that I say if I fender bend someone, PJ Tucker is the last person I want getting out of the other car. This means he is also the first person I want stepping out of my passenger seat. When the whistle stopped play in the third quarter, play continued. PJ Tucker stared six inches up to Kevin Durant and made himself bigger than he was. Any way you slice it these men were nose-to-nose. The physics of it don't make sense until you remember neither team had played in front of seventeen thousand fans before this game in over a calendar year. The players, coaches, and referees had stretched themselves out in empty arenas but now had to mind the fans when going for a loose ball or leaking out in transition. A simple, powerful prospect returned that night: they could be touched. Pressed in by strangers. Kevin Durant and PJ went nose-to-nose and a roar rose that hadn't since the world changed. And I may have never thrown a good punch in my life, but I served drinks on Water Street long enough to know how it made Kevin Durant look that once the roar went up his security guard leapt to the floor and shoved PJ Tucker.

To that point, it'd been over a year since I was in a room with more than ten people, and though the hoop was still ten feet tall it didn't look the same to anyone getting shots up that night. The Nets would never admit the crowd made a huge difference, but it did. The illness we'd been fighting that whole year required collective action that foregrounded the wellness of others, and that's not in our American bag. For those of us who feel mostly unexceptional, it takes more than five of us banded together to do the magical. And the crowd did just that.

One of the great improvements of Fiserv Forum over the Bradley Center is the verticality of the upper deck. The angle of the rows used to slope backward but now just go up and up. I like to think seventeen thousand voices pressing toward a court changes the flight of the ball just a bit, and when it's all concentrated on one man—one MVP of a man—and his personal bodyguard can't take it, it says the one thing the Bucks need it to trying not to go down 3-0: fear.

The Bucks won that night by three points but the fans won something else: we made a difference together for something we believed in. It'd been a long time since our athletic celebrities and their staff were reminded they weren't too different from us on a cellular level—something that can be transgressed in the wrong moment. And the thing about intimidation is even if it's benign—and we rely on security to ensure it is—the violence is already in their heads. And while I am a man averse to violence, I find myself attracted to this sort between the sidelines and what it means that a crowd could turn the fiction of a basketball game into something a little too real for a salaried security guard.

It'd been over a year since we've been able to talk about an arena as a fortress. It strikes me as odd that masculine rules prize not flinching in a duel when it's usually the first flinch that wins, but in the rarefied air of the world's greatest athletes I suppose my grade school coaches were right: the game is won and lost between the ears. And there are two types of teams that shoot 19% from three and eke out a win: a loser and a champion. With each passing game, the line between those fuzzed out of focus. None of the seventeen thousand fans in Fiserv Forum could make a shot in the NBA playoffs, and no player who wasn't named Giannis or Khris could either. But what the fans could do was nudge. Wherever that line is between loser and champion, I was either naive enough or optimistic enough or selfish enough to believe that together we could cover that distance. To have done the exceptional is intoxicating, and we would work to do it again and again for the head high of sharing a room together. Something that is binding is something that is real.

On the Southside God Is a Fact (Middleton v. Durant II)

TODAY I AM THINKING ABOUT WHERE fear and dread live in my body. Fear glows behind my eyes. It simmers. But dread is more acute, further away in my lungs. It waits for an exhalation and squeezes their lower thirds—dread reminds me there was once real estate there that is no longer available. It's more of a fact than uncertainty like fear. Fear feels imminent and either stays or passes into something else.

In Milwaukee, steeples rise like spikes over the cityscape. Especially on the southside, Catholic churches puncture generations of Dominican, Mexican, and Irish boundaries—sometimes it feels like you can't go more than six blocks without the fact of God following you around. For the Bucks, Kevin Durant is such a fact. He's going to get thirty, end of discussion—the defense just gets to choose how he does it and hope to keep him under forty.

Death, taxes, KD around and over you.

You'll have to forgive me for talking about game three to talk about game four, but there was a third-quarter stretch where the fact of Kevin Durant hit four back-to-back shots. And while you cannot sand the stone corners of a fact, Khris Middleton did what dread dares us not to: he made a fact of himself. KD scored twice, Khris fired back twice. But Khris's fact faltered—missed a twenty-footer—then KD came off a screen at the top of the key and nailed a three. Round 1: KD.

In the third quarter of game four, fear loomed larger in me than dread like Kevin Durant. Dread means I've accepted some certainty. Fear is a little worse. Fear with a jacket on can be mistaken for hope. And at some point, while I'd been lucky enough to be called "promising" in a few different ways, at some point you actually have to pay it off. And what I could never know for sure is the point at which fashioning myself as one of those Durant stone facts turned me into one—the moment a firework turns into a beacon of light—or how many days in a row you can be nothing before that's just what you are. It's the curse of belief—not knowing for sure.

I will admit I have asked many questions about Khris Middleton. In the final minute of the third quarter, Bobby Portis got a hand on a Kevin Durant entry pass. A rare error—turnover in progress, the court tilting the other way. Until Durant caught it himself and coolly nailed a baseline middie. 6.1 seconds remaining. A fact.

Then Khris Middleton called for the ball.

The clock started when the pass rose to his palm, and he put his damn head down. What I'll remember is the breakneck pace—Khris!—at which he moved down the left side of the floor. Mike Breen said, "Middleton drives and—"

With the grace of a flare singing its song, Khris stepped back. He fired over Joe Harris, Bruce Brown—even Kevin Durant himself—and sunk a three before the buzzer. Round 2: Middleton.

Khris did not run toward the bench to celebrate with open arms. Instead he turned away, lowered his head, and pumped a fist. He put the world on pause and stole the moment for himself. If we're keeping score—and we are—between Middleton's game three layup and this latest exchange, Middleton v. Durant is tied nine points to nine.

In the rarefied air of Kevin Durant, Khris Middleton caught his breath.

An Inventory of Wisconsin in My Portland Apartment

ONE BROOK LOPEZ SHIRSEY (BLACK)
One Cream City Giannis shirsey (green)
One cutting board in the shape of Wisconsin

One ice scraper in my trunk

One PBR bar key from my Nomad shifts

Two MKE Brewing Company pint glasses

One copy of *Shotgun Lovesongs* by Nick Butler

One Guided by Voices concert poster (9/1/2017; Turner Hall Ballroom)

One Muskego Parks and Rec tee ball team photo (circa 1999). The Red Sox. We had "Culver's" in bolded Arial font across our hats. My father coached us in jean shorts and a dark mustache. He knelt on the side.

For reasons around fading memories I only dimly understand, the longer I am away from home, the more I covet these items. There was a minute there when I was miserable in Madison where I took up minimalism. I donated or threw away three quarters of all my possessions. I liked the idea that nothing could be me or define me outside my physical self. A kind of raw individualism. I know better now—though not best—that the items that stayed are me too, as are some of the ones I gave away. In Madison, I was miserable enough to consider throwing myself away.

I think the years have made me just smart enough to know that if I'm not a different person day-to-day, I probably am month-to-month in small and perhaps ever-shrinking ways. But my brother's wedding above the Swinging Door Exchange is frozen in a picture frame, and so am I in all of these objects that are fast becoming relics. The thing about a photograph is its inevitability.

They take the ever-fraying threads of memory and tie them into a single rope of history. When I clean every so often, I dust these items first. This is the shape of comfort. My niece was five weeks old after Brooklyn game five, and I prefer being the only one not to meet her in three dimensions. There is something nice about being able to hold her without responsibility. Hold something real at bay while I do something else.

After game five, I cataloged my things in pursuit of the real American dream: destiny. More than a house, dog, and 2.5 kids. More than passive income. The American dream in Milwaukee is Bible-deep in the shape of accumulating capital—that everything we have done and will do both has and will continue to mean something on high. It was ordained long ago by whatever deities we worship that we are the ones who will prosper. The Catechism of the Catholic Church says, "The Church is at once holy and always seeking purification." In simpler terms: it is always right and it can save its sorries for later. Slavery, redlining, the housing bubble, the increasing gap between income and wealth—sorry, but today we're still golden. This is a religious American city's animating principle which means it is one of mine too.

I cataloged my things after game five because I wanted to know what I might give away if we lost one more game and Giannis decided to leave Milwaukee and win a championship somewhere else. I wanted to be prepared to throw some parts of myself away I deemed less than. This is how fickle self-love is—it didn't seem like such a bad thing. It's something we have practice in, the non-confrontational bunch that midwesterners are. I was ready to lose my histories and choose to be right—break my mirrors and forge onward. So goes the Church, so goes us all.

The easy promise of such certainty is as evil a thing I confess to craving in the tissue of my heart. Home holds me close in none of the ways I want to be held or behold but in all of the ways that tempt me. As if it couldn't follow me to the next city I "started over" in. As if it wouldn't haunt me.

They Built a Street Car and Buried It so They Could Build another Street Car

(PJ Tucker Will Write His Story and You Won't)

AFTER THE GAME, JIM OWCZARSKI OF the *Milwaukee Journal Sentinel* asked PJ Tucker about guarding Kevin Durant: "How do you think it's gone?"

The answer Jim was expecting—the one any good journalist on a deadline wants—was that of course it'd gone poorly. That Durant, in a single series, had reestablished himself as perhaps the best scorer on earth. But PJ saw through this, said he doesn't know why people are surprised Durant was playing so well. Owczarski tried again: "What have you enjoyed about this series? Obviously, there was that verbal altercation—the bodyguard thing—the intensity-type stuff. What have you sort of drawn from being able to be physical and kind of have all that?"

The question is full of promise at the beginning of phrases and vagueness to end them ("thing"; "-type stuff"; "kind of have all that?") because what Owczarski may have wanted to ask was uncomfortable. He wanted to hear how great KD was from a man whose win to force game seven just earned him the privilege of not prostrating before his opponent just this one time. I almost expected PJ to get mad. What he gave Jim Owczarski instead was not great for his deadline but a gift much greater than whatever story he was aiming for:

"It's the playoffs, man. Like, I don't know what people think…we dream about this our whole lives. I dream about being in the playoffs and guarding the best player in the world. I will die out there. I am living my dream. I'm not backing down from nothing. I'm fighting for every inch. I don't understand; everybody's like—all this little stuff—me and Kevin fight every year. I've guarded him every year during the playoffs. Golden State, Oklahoma City, it doesn't matter, regular season, playoffs. I love guarding him. I enjoy it. He's the best scorer I've ever seen in my life. I told [University of Texas Head Coach] Rick Barnes on his visit when he was a junior in high school, 'He's gonna be the best player I've ever seen in my life.' He killed us—I knew this—as an eleventh grader. I don't understand people. That's my brother. We compete. We fight every game. We're gonna fight again in game seven. It's part of it." Then PJ throws the vagueness and its gestures toward violence right back at the asker: "All that other stuff is just…stuff."

HEADING TOWARD THIRTY, I have been trying (and failing) lately to think less about people who would never give me an hour of their time or effort. To be specific: cleave people from the carousel of my mind I haven't seen in years or only met in passing. I have this belief there's something I'd know about myself if I wasn't too full of other people's opinions to see. And I don't know anyone in Milwaukee who likes riding the street car. For something that barely traverses 1% of the city's square mileage, it sure unites a lot of us that way. The rides have to be free because otherwise few would take them. And if belonging is a heaven, nothing is more golden to me than the road to it being paved with someone else's good intentions. Sometimes the solid we think we're doing someday is a different solid altogether. And sometimes the chore is the gift.

When I was younger and wild-eyed and weak, I didn't want to be a journalist anymore because I wanted to be that cliché: someone a journalist wrote about. These years later I'm trying not to see the conflation of validation and happiness as wasted time. Really trying. Here's my real secret: I think I'm supposed to be doing something great in this life—the kind of thing that affects thousands of people—and I still don't have the faintest fucking clue what it is. I'll admit how foolhardy it is to define oneself by impact on others versus starting with something more practical and healthy like, "Do I even enjoy living day-by-day?" But humans don't do well in isolation, and here I'm now on "dating" my third US city to find my people, and I'm starting to wonder if I ever actually loved my first love. And if God is when something goes awry and something good comes from it anyway, I'd like to state for the record my dislike of not being in control of this. I'm "bookish" in this specific way: I desire to have an explanation for everything that happens. It's a little emotionless and a little joyless. But it protects against surprise.

These days, I am trying to laugh a little more. Not defensively or by intellect like a walking *New Yorker* cartoon, but by waves of pure surprise that fill me before bubbling upward and out. I'm trying to laugh a laugh that takes up all the space of me. It's something I think evaporated between the loneliness of those first post-college years and a pandemic. Or maybe I left it in a basement at twelve years old pretending my computer speaker was a microphone and belting "Sugar We're Going Down" like the frontman of my own band at the Rave that just happened to play Fall Out Boy songs and nobody knew they were Fall Out Boy songs. That's what I wanted: to be the keystone of a room. A private wonder where I could fantasize about outsourcing my gratification.

PJ'S ANSWER SPREAD through Twitter in minutes and played on *SportsCenter* all night. The honesty came out poetic. One-on-one is the same way in neighborhood streets as it is under the spotlights, and it is in lowering his center of gravity in a dance to keep his feet in front of Kevin Durant's pivoting twister of a spin that PJ Tucker finds heaven. The score matters against someone else, but it does not matter when he is guarding Kevin Durant. This is a cosmic duel, and what a lightness that must be when you are an athlete whose success is defined by numbers and greatness finally escapes the commodification that always shackled it. It is this truth that makes me think the phrase "the whole is greater than the sum of its parts" is wrong, or at least it could be better. A team is made up of individuals chasing their own heavens, and that they happen to weave around and through each other is the happiest accident. Is this not the real miracle of a place we call "home?" It's what goodness—the real and true kind—looks like. Maybe the sum of parts close together is greater than the sum of parts that never touch.

I imagine down the years we will focus on PJ Tucker saying he will die out there against Kevin Durant. But PJ told Eric Nehm something else that night that has ever since periodically demanded my attention. What are the odds that across decades of work—across continents—that PJ Tucker and Kevin Durant find their heavens together? The reward is a time warp—a warm glow I can only remember from childhood.

Tell me if you've heard something like this before. Perhaps you've lived it: Durant got close to PJ and said, "Stop fighting with Blake. You're gonna get thrown out. And then we can't play."

I Would Like to Give Coach Bud One (1) Flower

...IF I HAD ONE TO SPARE.

When you're not taking the shot, you usually won't get the credit—this is for you, Bud:

Kevin Durant scored more points than anyone in the history of game sevens. No one will remember that he went 0-6 in overtime, and if they remember even one of those shots, it'll be the last one over Jrue that looked on line and ready to end a season before falling short. KD played every minute of that basketball game, and 336 into the series with five to go, his body's gas light came on.

It is rare in 2024 that austerity earns acclaim, but I want Coach Bud to know I saw him. Coach Bud trusted the science and the math. He took care of his players' bodies, and that's why when the game extended ten-percent after regulation: the Bucks pressed the accelerator instead of praying cruise control would get them to the next exit. Coach Bud could not save his players, but he put them in a place where they could save themselves. He was no fisher of men, though—he was a man of conviction who was proven—singularly, and then a few weeks later, all at once—correct. He had not only believed in "play random" or the drop defense or in limiting minutes—he had believed that no matter how loud the whispers got about his job security or how clearly his eyes might tell him to start taking away the three that in the sliver of space between his sternum and his heart there was chain-mail belief in himself. Perhaps this is what it means to love our people: that we define our success by others, but we still count ourselves among them.

And in this moment a few years later I am discovering this is one of the ways I am truly stunted and maybe had done the stunting myself. I embraced for so long that which taught me to distrust myself: my religion. I spent nearly three decades trying to be Christ-like and am in my first truly trying to be Ben-like. For so long, my worth had been in giving: being nice and then being liked as a result of being nice. When I was eleven I saw my family spreading apart, and I held much of it together with the Scotch tape and paperclips of getting in the way when my brothers drew my mother's ire and filling cement-hard silences with any small talk nicety I could to soften the air. Somehow, it worked. This is something I do not regret and would never change—but what I can't accept is the narcotic high that kind of power and external sense of morality gave me. I went about my life for almost thirty years trying to be nauseatingly exceptional in the eyes of others: I drove that motorcycle, worked as a Racing Sausage for the Brewers, drafted a novel, played in a good band, got trim and fit, started tending bar, and read as many smart books as I could. I enjoyed each of these things independently, I think, but the admiration they won me from acquaintances who probably didn't think about me for months at a time cobbled together my mosaic of who I was. What I cannot accept is going any longer without finally taking at least a few cues from myself. It's not that there's some dormant version of me finally awakening, but my soul has spent too long reading instructions on how and when to pull my own levers. It might mean some kind of starting over, but I thought I already did that leaving Wisconsin. I just didn't get anywhere.

It is in this way I would like to be more like Coach Bud, but I don't yet know how. What about myself do I know for certain that no one will ever touch no matter how loud the whispers grow? I would have been Steve Nash any other year and perhaps this one too: played Giannis, Khris, and Jrue as close to forty-eight minutes as they would let me. I would have lost, and my team would have discarded me and never thought about me again. Milwaukee doesn't think about me now one iota as much as I think about it and its people. I don't know that I'd call it a fantasy (probably more like a compulsion)—it's something that's alive in my head but perpetually around the year I left. Milwaukee is no longer that place. I am holding fast to a memory as though it is currency in the present. It is not quite worthless. It is its own kind of purgatory.

I do not have a flower to give Coach Bud. But I owe him one—for the difference between being nice and being kind: being okay with refusing compromise. A defense mechanism tells me that foregrounding myself like this is a Libertarian value—here I am trying to be liked again—but I think it's a pretty severe oversight at almost thirty that I do not know what it means to trust myself. My own body is warning me against knowing, as though there's something to face before I can earn that trust. But I think I would like to know.

It would be merciful to know.

Conference Finals:

Atlanta Hawks

Trae Young Is Unstuck in Time

IF YOU CATCH TRAE YOUNG AT A standstill with the ball—and pity poor you—you're in danger. The world you are wishing for is not the one you will inhabit at the end of the game. Trae Young is living proof it is neither better nor worse to be feared than respected—they can be the same thing.

Perhaps more than any other sport, there is a collective rhythm about basketball. There's a washing of waves up and down the floor and the elastic stretch of a rebounder finding a guard for an outlet pass into the fast break. And I must respect—which means I must fear—a man who never releases his elastic end and plants himself until he tears the fabric of the game.

With 2:24 left in the third quarter, Jrue Holiday was fully over a John Collins screen toward the right wing where the whole floor tilted when Trae crossed back over. The other nine players slid downstream, Trae set his feet before the three-point line, and he waited. Alone.

I mean it when I tell myself the body is an instrument and not an ornament, but that is something far easier to believe in my head than in my bones. The mirror has only ever been my enemy as I'm sure it is many of yours, but I am not disgusted by the way I look as much as underwhelmed. Into adulthood, my mother polices my food portions in public without knowing it, and I'll put down the food and spiral lightly. What incenses me more in hindsight is how little of a difference those decades of smaller portions ever made to how I think about how I look. It's something she'd done and then I practiced myself for almost thirty years to no discernible success. Oh, what I'd give to just be whelmed instead of somehow seeing someone nearly 6'2 as eternally stubby. I do not think people look at me with disgust but instead with something worse—no feeling at all.

This was Jrue Holiday's twelfth year, and he was now away from Trae on the complete wrong side of the court. This possession, he accepted defeat. So too had Bobby Portis, in his seventh year, waiting patiently in the lane for the open three to go up. Jrue and Bobby had seen enough of this shit in their careers. There's a resignation about it: just one of tens of thousands of possessions. This one's done—on to the next. Depending on how close you are to the game you might call for Trae waiting to shoot rather than contesting the shot something like "respect." Trae had seized every defender. And yet, he waited.

Say what you will about the virtues of an instrument and the limitations of an ornament, no sound can twist in the light the way an ornament can. I have always loved people in motion. People running less so—too focused for my taste—but anything with a mindlessness of life to it: filling a watering can, turning a paperback page, checking a blind spot. There is a fullness in watching cars pass driven by people who are always and forever themselves in the tiniest of ways. Newness does not impress me. I do not want attention—to be clear: I crave validation—but absent that, I want you to be you. A musician who wields an instrument will tell you that much of what makes beauty is, in fact, a science: study and practice inching toward perfection. But from the curled edge of a Christmas tree limb, an ornament does its own talking.

Then: The shrug. People called it a shimmy, but a shimmy is something set to a beat, an expulsion of energy. A shrug is an attempt to find the place your shoulders used to sit before your heart welded stress into your body. And it was in this moment Trae Young refused momentum. It would have carried a shot toward the rim at the pace of the game's smooth metronome. Instead, he redefined it. It was not his hair or his gangly upper body who was out-of-step just standing while seconds ticked off the shot clock. It was a sold-out arena, coaches and staff, twenty-nine other players, and millions from home including myself who were. Our eyeballs drifted toward the hoop for a shot that wasn't there.

When he was good and ready, he drained the three, and as the Bucks inbounded the ball again, Trae stood still. Everyone else washed by.

Envy presses outward from my chest when I think about such confidence. I wonder how much Trae thinks about his thinning hair at all. This is perhaps closer to what I imagine happiness to be: operating at one's own singular, deliberate pace with little regard for how others see them. How freeing that must be. Ninety-nine other players could have crossed over, shimmied, and hit a three, but ninety-nine players never did.

I am writing this in the morning, and I am now on to my third hair product and pretty exhausted of it—after the salt spray, after a pre-blow-dry gel with a medium hold, now I'm rubbing hair clay that smells of sweet tobacco into my palms and running it through my hair. The blow dryer comes hot and low over my scalp. I lift my hair brush up and back, up and back trying to find that volume and shine my barber did but I can never replicate. This is a ritual without any of the peace of a ritual. At the end, I always think of a photograph of me at four years old. How blond I was then versus how the color has left it now. The cowlick at four years old summited my whole head, and I realize it's this color and this shape, not what the barber did, that I've been chasing ever since I can remember. My hair is short around the sides now because I am told this looks good on men. And this, I guess, is where Trae Young and I are the most different. To notice Trae Young's flaws is to be in danger—to underestimate. For you basketball fans, I pray that you never have the time to notice Trae Young's hair during a game for your team's own good, and for my own: I pray you never notice who I am isn't quite who I used to be or who I imagined I'd become after some years away. There is a singular benefit to being feared: demanding such a distance. No one in their right mind would ever sit you upright and press their fingers against your chest to see what sounds you make.

Damned If You Do; Really Damned if You Don't (A Love Song)

GIANNIS ANTETOKOUNMPO SIZES YOU UP
and backs a few more feet behind the three-point line.
He is going to drive. Do you, the defender, meet him at

the three-point line to slow his momentum? Or back up to the key to give yourself more time to read whether his feet will go around (or through) you? (If you meet him at the three-point line, skip to the next paragraph). The neat trick of the eye is a 6 '11 man does not only run at you, but he grows in every direction as he does. This is, of course, impossible, so you widen your stance and lower your center of gravity. You absorb his body blow and air spurts out of your mouth. With all the power of a semi-truck, Giannis spins. A single twist of a dime balancing itself on a kitchen table.

Giannis is past you. Now leave your body and become the help defender. You're equally as tall as Giannis and even have a few pounds on him. Giannis is barreling at the rim, but you've expected this. With Giannis, you always expect this. It already happened before he ever took that first stride toward the lane. It was always going to happen.

THE NUMBER IS 231. The date is January 31, 2019.

This was my weight when I told the woman I'd been fawning over in grad school that if we couldn't be together, I didn't think we should be friends. We'd already road tripped to Arizona together, taught each other the card games we learned as kids, made pad Thai.

It was winter in Texas but strangely warm. Dark outside. We walked through a hilly park by a river and I explained I just wanted a chance, and I needed to draw this boundary for my own health. I couldn't keep donating time and thought to someone who wouldn't reinvest it in me. I felt like a man saying these things.

She was seeing someone else, she said. And then she cried that I would leave like this.

Later, I realized this was something of a superpower: I could break up with women who didn't even like me. I told many people this in the story afterward.

DO YOU RISE TO MEET Giannis and sacrifice your body—force to force—taking away the dunk and forcing a pass? Of course you do. Your defense is already scrambling to rearrange itself like a slide puzzle to cover the man you left. And now: success. Giannis crashes into you, and your hands are so far up that you touch the ball with both hands.

You're straight up. It's a clean block. This is what it takes to stop a supernova.

THE NUMBER IS 180 FLAT. The date is April 5, 2019.

It happened. That night we got together and spent the morning ordering tacos from my bedroom and talking.

Intermittent fasting was what I called it, but in hindsight losing fifty pounds in around two months was probably a little bit of that and a lot of starvation. It appealed to the zealot in me who found more respect for the commitment some religions and spiritualities required than the all-you-can-eat-but-at-least-eat-something buffet of my Catholic upbringing. And as a grad student with few responsibilities before 2pm any day, I could afford to eat a late dinner and sweat the next sixteen hours. Many days I napped the final hour or two rather than deal with the gnawing hunger. Aha! A life hack!

Some days, if I'm honest, the sixteen hours stretched into eighteen. I congratulated myself.

Here's the kicker: I'm actually one for a good food binge. Until January of this year I'd spent almost eighteen straight months eating an entire frozen pizza once a week (the key is to sprinkle Italian seasoning over the top on its way into the oven and drizzle BBQ sauce over it after slicing but before it cools). Food is a form of mindfulness for me. It centers, and this is something only I can know.

We left the pool hall at bar close and kissed in the alley. I had my months-long Rocky workout montage, and I was finally enough.

Nevermind that it hadn't occurred to me then and wouldn't for years that it was the confident person I'd become drawing personal boundaries that got her to see me in a new way. It's not the first time I've left toxicity, thrived, and ran back thinking I was the problem all along and I'm finally ready to have everything I've ever wanted.

That first night at the pool hall, I played "This Life" by Vampire Weekend on the jukebox. It's a song she loved on our road trip months earlier. Our eyes barely missed each other across the tables. Twenty minutes later, I heard "El Scorcho" by Weezer start up. We played it over and over. The prettiest woman in a small Texas town told me she loved me. It made me feel safe. This was my movie, and I'd earned it.

A year later on the day of my thesis defense, I got a job offer in Portland, a little over an hour from her parents. We stuffed a Budget truck with our things and headed on a three-day drive to the northwest. The truck didn't have cruise control. Except for a four-hour stretch from New Mexico into Utah where my calf cramped, I drove every mile. During the stops I found cheap hotels on Hotwire. We spent one night in Albuquerque and another north of Salt Lake City. We were supposed to stop a third night, but I couldn't help competing against myself—I powered through thirteen hours of driving the last day and pulled up to our new apartment. It had a balcony and birdsong.

YOU PRESS AT THE BALL—reject its advance toward the rim—but the ball is gone. You and Giannis are still falling when the ball is cradled fully under and past your left hand. It rolls into the hoop. He'd done the impossible. This was always going to happen.

2008. FRESHMAN YEAR of high school.

My mother yelled at my brothers again in their distant corners of the house. The sound came as it did from so deep in her stomach it was percussive. It rattled the dishes in the glass cabinets.

Our house was built to host, designed to be entered through the front door, adorned with stained glass on its sides into a foyer—"foy-ay," Mom told me—with a black, pointed chandelier I always avoided standing beneath for fear it just might skewer me. We entered through the garage into the laundry area, its floors perpetually dusted with salt stains from Wisconsin winters. As kids, we ran right downstairs. It wasn't so much a matter of preference for our thick television that shocked our fingers when we turned it on, but international borders. We claimed the basement and my mother claimed the first floor, which made the kitchen hers. Our father worked too early and late and far away to claim anything. Kids owned the second-floor bedrooms, but the non-negotiable crucifixes and tableware ban made them feel contested. In the wrong moment, to be in my mother's territory meant feeling a kind of danger.

My father was traveling because he was stuck loving us unconditionally and my mother was home because she was stuck doing the same. In six years, I'd know she was doing her best as a parent. But that morning when the glass settled I chose to negotiate space where my brothers needed to isolate. I was not a pro at this—while she stewed in the kitchen all I could do was fall to the living room couch and fight my legs' flight response. She was maybe fifteen feet away, but we could feel each other's presence.

The TV was on, and only we could see it. I turned the volume down. I was making space for her without looking at her. It was too little to solve anything. This was a kind of apology unique to our region's way of life: where if we can hold or be held even in just our peripheries it is space we'll appreciate and we won't ask for more. It was also love as best I could show, as best as she could, as best as any of us could.

No, Khris's handle isn't loose; he just scored 38.

ELEVEN REBOUNDS, I SAID TO MYSELF, breathing through it. Yes, he turned the ball over four times, but he scored thirty-eight points—a series MVP performance by any other name. And yet I've got that electricity in my neck calling for criticism. The thing is when failures are so spectacular they're easy for the armchair fan like myself to latch on to. Case in point, Khris chucking the ball directly off the backboard. Charitably, you'd call it a failed lob for Brook Lopez who was still busy posting up Clint Capela. More practically: it looked like a moment in a video game where you press the wrong button. Failures happen a thousand ways—some of Khris's are just plain loud. Never do I consider, though, that Brook should have been there. Khris threw the pass with such force it telegraphed he felt the play obvious. And the thing about Khris Middleton is he always sees the floor. And I paced in my living room seeing a Corona commercial. We are not the same.

Defenders know the one way to beat Khris Middleton is to get up into him. Hurrying him is the best strategy. I am aware—which in the realm of real hoop heads means I am dimly aware—that Khris's mistakes are not brain "dead" as much as they are brain "full." When Khris isn't rushed he can almost sashay to his spots off the elbow for a jumper or a quick pocket pass to Giannis. His favorite way to dribble and see the floor is to shield the defender with his body, keep his dribble low, and turn his head. Long-armed defenders trouble Khris because as he surveys the court the ball comes up a little higher each dribble, a little more available. The ball hits his palm low and then his palm rises with the ball. Every dribble becomes a binary choice for Khris: is the time now? Yes or no. And every time he runs out of time to ask, he needs his teammates' help to act.

In 2021, I'd thought when he hurried his way into a steal it'd been his fault, but now I know Khris wishes his teammates shared his urgency in those moments. He would never cry for help, but how do his teammates not see it when he can see them so clearly? This is the kind of prison empathy can put you in. I walk around with something of an ego, but I still like to think I'm about average in most things. How's my sleep? Same as everyone else. How's my mental health? About average.

It is perhaps this that when our world faces yet another in a series of colossal failures that it becomes so maddening—the lack of ability of people we break bread with or share space with or open doors for to see what we know is plain. I like to think I'm not the only one where empathy can easily roll into resentment. I'm known by myself to frequently rehash things I'd wish I'd said in an argument or conduct, in my head, an entirely fictional argument altogether. For resentment and empathy can want the same thing: fairness.

I expect someone with the vision of Khris Middleton to spring his teammate open. I do not expect Bobby Portis to both create the space for and then find the corner shooter. And yet: Giannis doesn't roll strong to the near block and the pocket pass gets deflected and it's Khris who threw it. Khris has to curl the ball into his chest and wave a teammate to cut, and it's full seconds before they do. We want fairness in this binary, but people—even the excellent ones we revere—are rather flawed, clumsy beings who happened to figure out how to build skyscrapers. We will not get it with machine perfection. We are not the same people who wandered forty years in the desert on faith alone. I prefer a map with a straight line to paradise and I've trusted our leaders to have one folded in their back pocket.

It is the easy and prideful thing to simplify the world but what we are simplifying is people, and it can be the good decisions we've made that can unravel us the next. There is a safety in feeling the intensity of this within the rectangular box of a televised sporting event, but the emotions are real. I think it's fair for us to treat them as such because if a nation or a teammate refuses to become more perfect, the occasional frustration with Khris's game is the place we can start is ourselves.

Conference Finals: Game 15, Loss, 88-110 (2-2)

(Untitled)

IT'S A DIFFICULT THING TO WATCH A man known for his physical dominance be tender with himself, and Giannis Antetokounmpo held his knee the way you'd hold a butterfly.

When something is wrong there are several ways to circle the differences between the picture of how a scene should be and the scene of how it is, but what I can't get out of my head is the way he folded his body. Giannis for the first time looked small and the Bucks lost their will and PJ Tucker said it best after the game because he couldn't say anything: "We still gonna win. This is not how this series is going to go, because this can't be how... like I gotta..."

YOU CAN BE BEATEN by surprise or you can save yourself some time to be beaten exactly how you know you will be.

MY PARTNER QUIT HER NEW Portland job the first day—a terrible shift in a foster home that needed hands. We found her a solid car, but after the test drive I learned her credit score was so bad she needed a guarantor. I called my dad to ask if I should do it, and he told me, "do what you feel is right." I refused to sign. The next day I bought my own car with help from my family and I resented her for not being able to take care of herself.

We slept in one bedroom and the other was for her craft work and a television. In week two, she started closing the door.

In week four we stopped touching.

AND I GUESS IN THIS NEW and promising city I chose surprise, although the way I ached then and now for home in all its dimensions makes me wish I'd known better to leave, or at least have had better information. I think about cradling my niece and whispering the one fairy tale I know until she sleeps, and I think about how the next time I hug my parents will be one of a dwindling number of hugs I'll ever get, and I will count those hugs and after I leave I'll pretend my seat back on the plane is where their hands might meet to feel them just one more time. They have been together thirty-five years, and I wonder now how large of an impact I ever had on any relationship into its fourth decade or that we ever made it as a family. I know as a kid I thought about it, and I recognize that early sense of self-importance. But I don't bargain to know the answer. What we have now are holidays and meals we enjoy and close relationships by our own standards that couldn't have been fathomed years earlier.

I hug my brothers now when I can. We grew up in suburbs but without consulting each other we each chose to claim our years in Milwaukee as our lives. And even though we don't hug tight, we hug as best as we can. And we do it in the city.

Ode to Labor

ON MAY 5, 1886, WISCONSIN STATE MILITIA looked down from the Bay View rolling mill on one thousand striking workers and fired.

Workers had shut down every business in town to strike for an eight-hour workday except the mill, and they marched for this very last holdout. The militia acted on orders of the governor and scattered workers for cover—except the fallen. Seven people including a child. And the workers persisted. They organized and attacked a weak governor. Milwaukee elected Daniel Hoan, who later made the cover of *Time* in 1936 with an article calling his Milwaukee "one of the best run cities in the U.S." A bridge bearing his name now stretches from Bay View to downtown. Milwaukee is the first and also the last major city to elect a Socialist mayor. It has been many places in the last sixty years, and now 140 years after the Bay View Massacre, I am thinking about the commitment to getting that last business closed. Hundreds had already won, but we don't forget our brothers and sisters. We are always acting for our brothers and sisters.

Brook Lopez's teammates in the Disney bubble called him Brooklyn Brook referring to his dynamic post-up days as the all-time leading scorer in Nets franchise history. And as nice as that is, I imagine it was tough to swallow the dry celery of teammates wanting you to be who you were years ago—that Milwaukee Brook wasn't good enough. And the ask itself was impossible. We are not time travelers. By 2021, Brook wore a lifting belt on the bench to protect his lower back. You wouldn't say he did much with what you would call "speed." But in game five against the Hawks, Brooklyn Brook found his way to the surface.

With just two minutes left in the fourth quarter, Brooklyn Brook and Milwaukee Brook fused in a perfect play. Brook received the ball in the lane with his back to the basket. Maybe in a younger year a different Brook might've jumped before seeing the hoop, but this one was a hair more patient or maybe uncertain. These possessions mattered in a way his years toiling in Brooklyn didn't. His last toe stayed grounded until he turned to the rim. Not much air. Brook faded away—pushed the ball more than he shot it—and when it left his hand for his thirtieth point it was Brooklyn Brook's fingertips that floated the balance of touch and air and spin. The rest of his body, though, churned slow. It's an old head who doesn't just know where the hoop is but where everyone else on the floor is without having to look. Giannis might not have torn his ACL, so that night I did my best to be grateful for what I could. And that night Brook Lopez needed both who he used to be and who he is to be the best version of himself.

Over a lifetime we are all several different people, but that night proved when we become someone new we don't lose who we used to be. Maybe turning the page doesn't mean turning forward or back, but that sometimes when your loved ones need it you tear the page out, fold it a few times, and stick it under the leg of a wobbly dinner table.

It is easy to be afraid we aren't who we once were, and it is even easier to be frustrated by knowing in some years we are still only some vague notion of who we'd one day like to be. We contain multitudes, yes, and games like this make me thank God that's true. Each of these players lived in Milwaukee. They parked their cars and walked the same potholed streets we did. They could smell the Miller barley when the wind carried it from the valley. For every eight hours of work in the arena or the gym, they had eight hours of rest and eight hours of what they pleased. They carried this city and its history with them everywhere they went and everywhere they will go the rest of their lives as champions. When Brook's last leg left the ground on that late shot, he was jumping off a piece of hardwood over concrete over wires over concrete over dirt that was millions of people in the making. And that night I like to think his brethren going back a hundred years pressed him just another quarter inch in the air.

I would like to stake my reputation on the cream city brick upon which this city and its team is built, but I can't. What I can endorse, though, is an attitude: to have lost someone great, said "fuck you," and come around to winning a different way—Khris Middleton grabbed thirteen rebounds, Jrue Holiday dished thirteen assists, and Bobby Portis notched three steals. Brook Lopez scored thirty-three points without Giannis and perhaps no one knows better than an identical twin like him that neither Brooklyn nor Milwaukee Brook could have done this on their own.

So may we all.

Solidarity forever.

Bucks in Six (Movin' Out)

THE DAY OF THIS GAME, SIX WEEKS INTO moving to a new city with my partner, I told her that lately it'd been like we're friends and maybe that's for the best and it's Holiday for three and where does the joy of basketball come from—it's an exchange and Tony Snell deserved better than the Hawks and I opted into being alone and for the first time in forever my brain was awash in the pink warmth of a prophecy fulfilled and Khris Middleton had an answer whenever you posed a question and the suburban mom sign that says "Happiness is a journey not a destination" is still wrong (it seems such a waste of time if that's what it's all about) I just know it's not this and Atlanta really let itself believe before remembering who they were that year and the Bucks were back in the finals for the first time in fifty years and my home and I evolved in parallel and whatever is correlation or causation is still synchronicity and lighting starts in the

floor and demands the sky and maybe happiness is the
pure else of something, knowing I am not done *doing*, and
that unending promise is written inside fresh pull tabs
but my world for these weeks became a symphony not
just a single sound. It wasn't a coda. It was an intro that
would play for my lifetime: a Jrue stepback—intoxication
following change sounds more like addiction—a Khris
baseline fadeaway—my favorite love is a selfish one—Pat
Connaughton finding a new way to get hit in the face—I
was never one city nor another I was something else
I needed to learn to accept—Bobby flex—I could die
and the world wouldn't change; I would change—the
Bratzooka!—my city died seven years ago I am gone
I am—Ice(d) Trae—I have nothing it needs—cause
Brandon Jennings foretold—

this is only a sound—"And one!"—where I must be a
believer—Light it up! Light it up!—

In what I've carried with me across time zones—I will
die out there—

And I will only know my people—pick—

By the size—pass—

Of their echo—

Bucket—

NBA Finals:
Phoenix Suns

Parlor Trick

BASKETBALL IS VERTICAL UNLESS YOU'RE Chris Paul, who—I have to note—is small. He's six feet if he stands all the way up. Not particularly long. But set a screen for Chris Paul and watch all five defenders tense. Getting Chris Paul into a twist with your starting center is a dance you lose every time. With all the same pace he runs straight ahead, Paul roves across the entirety of the lane waiting a full twenty seconds for the big to lunge forward. Or that's how it feels—really he can feel the vibrations of every movement around him. To be on the floor against Chris Paul—or now his protégé Devin Booker—is to feel the tensity of guarding Chris Paul one-on-one even when you're on another man. Chris Paul is small and I am grateful because Chris Paul is my favorite parlor trick. What looks extraordinary at first and then is impressive. The ordinary that becomes extraordinary is magic.

Chris Paul had been doing this parlor trick for sixteen years across five teams and all thirty NBA cities. Like every great trick, it's not magic, really—it is practiced and it is refined. There are no secrets to what Chris Paul is doing, negotiating the invisible strings he has on all five defenders and the pulley systems rigged up to his feint and his crossover—teams have been running the pick and roll for decades. It is an old technology. If you ask NBA historians, there have been at least four permutations of entire basketball strategy in the last 50 years—whole championship playbooks solved by defenses and shredded. None of them have solved the pick and roll. What Chris Paul does is timeless. But I need to say: the one thing he doesn't have is time itself. At that moment, Paul was in his first NBA Finals at age 36, and what I don't understand is how he remained so patient on the floor. I couldn't drive a car when Chris Paul started to devote his career to winning an NBA championship. Thousands of hotel room beds. Tens of thousands of reps holding himself back, waiting for the moment his screener's feet set.

Even then, Paul waits to pinprick the balloon of a defense. Mostly, he waits until they do it themselves—tens of thousands of reps, and yet they always do. Chris Paul shredded defenders the same way after 9/11 as he does in a pickup run as he does with one finger on the trophy he's spent two decades seeing in his dreams. No momentum carries him forward in the way it would carry me—he has the patience of a glacier. And perhaps too the focus of one. Chris Paul as a competitor isn't too different from the TV show *Severance*—he drops his personal history the moment he steps on the floor, or if he doesn't, its singularity has been obscured by almost two decades of repetition. Chris Paul worked at his grandfather's gas station, the first Black-owned gas station in North Carolina. Chris committed to Wake Forest, and the next day his grandfather died. Chris Paul goes back to North Carolina, but it's not quite "home"—he lives outside of LA in Encino. When the curtains open and the spotlight narrows, Chris Paul turns it on. Chris Paul the basketball player carries with him what he can fit in his carry-on, and Giannis brings his family. He cannot separate the two—who he was growing up around his family and who he is as a basketball player, and his brother Thanasis is at his side on the bench every game. It is not that there is no separation between personal Giannis and the professional one, but that the professional one springs forth from his history, from his family. Chris Paul dedicates much of his life away from his basketball uniform to justice, but what's inside the lines is born inside the lines, lives inside the lines, and will die there too. And when it does, there will be a life beyond it—something to reintroduce himself to but something to return to. And in a life well-lived is this separation better? I worry for Giannis when basketball goes away. I worry for any cleaving that takes a blade down an undefined path.

What I think I am trying to write about here is again momentum, what carries us in the directions we go, and what boundaries we choose to respect for ourselves. Chris Paul's belief in unions and the pursuit of whatever shade of justice he believes in will carry him long after he stops rounding his screener, but on the court of his life he can stop on a dime. Something bogs me down when I try to pivot and sprint somewhere new. Maybe the thousands of hotel rooms are really a gift—the only constant in a sixteen-year NBA career is yourself. I have lived in just three cities in my adult life and I'm still learning how to learn to love where I am as a way of loving who I am, not who I'd like to be or who I like that I've already been. This is lonelier than I am comfortable with, and I am still learning—so I've been caught picking up my dribble again. It is time to reset again. And go.

I Don't Mind Being Dead I Just Mind the Dying

WE NEVER GOT TO SEE KURT COBAIN make a bum record. There were no years he got all into jazz or DMT—he never aged into a different era. And I don't think it's too dark to say that the brief and perfect sample we have of him plays a role in why we love him so much. How neat and contained his music feels—either perfect or incomplete. Longing is so often the base for a love. What we crave is more time with who we had gotten to know, not loving him for the freedom of who he would have become. Everything we think about how

Kurt Cobain would view the decades since his death or how he might comfort us after a breakup is fanfiction. It doesn't make those nights between our headphones unreal—they are very real—it's just what I mean when I say I don't mind being gone, I just mind the pain of my leaving.

We lost the first two games of the Finals, and most of what I remember now about the feeling is how it was a bad look for the city. Camera crews were finally broadcasting from the riverwalk or in front of the Calatrava, and it reminded them we never belonged. Or worse: that they never thought about us at all and they're reminded why.

Did Stephen A. Smith want to travel to Milwaukee? "Hell no," he said. Molly Qerim called it a "terrible city." ESPN shipped a whole operation from a more desirable coast to the Deer District and no doubt they were hoping for the Bucks to lose and make it a short stay. I have never and will never meet these people, and I still felt slighted. This is—I think—what it means that I and the place that made me are addicted to being nice: our mayor sent Stephen A. and Molly gift baskets. *See? We're not mad; we just want you to give us a chance. We're extending a hand because this is the destiny we've been waiting for and there's room for you too.* Our relevance was the greater good made manifest. We would have meant something. The alternative? It's what millennials figured out with social media, what anyone in a small city has known for a hundred years: not being seen is a kind of suffering. And we didn't want to hurt anymore.

I have to call us back from one loss to another: to the game everyone but Giannis thought he tore his ACL. It was the first time I can remember Giannis looking small, and PJ Tucker said it best after the game because he couldn't say anything: "We still gonna win. This is not how this series is going to go because this can't be how… like I gotta…"

We might all want to be the main characters in our own story, but the math says almost none of us are the subject of *the* story—it is humiliating to discover you are not Cinderella; you are somebody at the ball whose name will never be recorded. We choose to believe we might be anyway. And I am not immune to this American strain of destiny—it led me to teaching three years of high school trying to single-handedly alter the course of each student's life through the uncut power of old books and care. The only way I've ever known how to feel safe is to feel necessary—to be on people's minds. But tonight and every other night, Milwaukee is writing its story without me at a comfortable cadence. It's finishing its sentences one day, hour, and second at a time. And looking back now, moving away I told everyone that I was going to explore other parts of the US, but really I just wanted to be the prodigal son. I didn't care for Milwaukee on its own terms—I cared for me. I saw Milwaukee as broken and, in some delusion, thought I might carve out my own place as someone who changed it for the good. But I didn't really love Milwaukee. I wanted to love myself. And after getting a failing grade I blamed the pencil rather than the speller.

But the truth is it was only after leaving the state that I started watching every single Bucks game I could. I took it with me all the way down to Texas and then to Oregon. And we are separate—myself and the city that helped build me—but we are not untethered, and all I could do was say I loved Milwaukee while also hating it a little because I say I love myself but also hate him a little too.

IF I WAS DYING RATHER than dead it'd be a real fucking drag for some good people, and I've been passing mirrors for at least the last twenty years but never once considered how it'd be a drag for me. Here is the God complex I've crowdsourced, and I like to imagine I'm not alone: that my presence and happiness makes this world a better place than I'd found it. I've made my tiny changes to earth. Many of us have.

This is a rosy thought, and it is also one I do not like much. I think about my world as a room I'm cleaning for someone else, not my own place where I can kick my feet onto the coffee table. This is the definition of nice. It is progression without any pleasure. It is not kindness.

I'd like to get rid of all my mirrors. Not smash them but pluck them right off the wall, walk them down my building's stairs and lean them against the dumpster. I have never not sucked in my gut in front of a mirror. It first happened when I was six or seven and aware of my weight and it never stopped. The damned things don't seem to work—over twenty years in front of these things and I've never honestly seen myself. I'd like to quiet quit being perceived—just enough to get by. Be done with being perceived by the friends, exes, former coworkers, and family whose names and faces and memory wisps scroll across my mind every day taking me somewhere I no longer am.

It may be fair to call tying one's identity to a city or the moral clarity of sport an addiction rather than a love, but the two are close.

I cast my body someplace new and now I have to reel myself in. My city cannot teach me kindness, cannot teach me mercy. Nice isn't enough. I am the only one who can teach myself to plunge where I've only dipped to my ankle. I remember kindness's name—we've met in passing more than a few times. I have held a door open for it. Safe to say we are acquaintances. If I see it on the street, I'd say, "hi there" and try to keep 'er moving. Love is so personal it is a handprint in wet concrete, all of a person's tiny topographies pressed into permanent goo. I may not yet be old enough to be set in my ways, but concrete hardens over time. I must press for myself while I can.

Bobby

MY BROTHER AND SISTER-IN-LAW MOVED to the suburbs, and their surprise at me ringing the doorbell the day before game three let me know this was the kind of house where family ought to just walk in.

We'd scored some tickets to the game and I moved my life for it. My niece was two months old.

Babies are either terrified of my large head or find it fascinating; but when I cradled Kaylee she broke into a soft smile before leveling it out and breaking one again like she was thinking of a fond memory over and over. Courtney coached me on how to hold her because I was too stiff about it. I'd held her peeking over my shoulder—a far less familial position—but Kaylee liked this too. We had things in common, you see: we both appreciated a good set of kitchen cabinets and the modern ceiling fan. While gravity pulled at the bags under my brother and sister-in-law's eyes, I couldn't help sharing bewilderment at everything Kaylee managed to do. A smarter man than me once sang, "how strange it is to be anything at all," and the sheer wonder of her existence moment-to-moment filled my brother's house with an airy lightness. Every laugh, arm wave, or hiccup was wonderful. There's a shared momentum around her—we all silently understood that her happiness came first and the rest was gravy. And what is belonging if not silent understanding in sync.

Their suburban silo was a welcome change from the city that was a different hue than the one I'd left four years before. Not bad, just different. Or maybe I was.

Let me say some of the obvious: the Deer District really did have ten thousand outside the arena, Fiserv Forum was loud (I don't care what that podcast from *The Ringer* said), and Gucci Mane was really there (voluntarily!). Less obvious was how good I felt being a tourist in my hometown. It's a real question whether friendships that have become once-every-second-months friendships could turn back into once-a-week friends. John Darnielle on his podcast *I Only Listen to the Mountain Goats* said the places we live are just reflections of who we are at that moment, and I small-talked a dozen or so friends and struggled to find our old rhythms. It worked for a few, but old times are old. The cool restaurants I knew were either closed or city mainstays, and the cool restaurants then were ones I'd never heard of.

In Fiserv Forum, Bobby Portis's name rang like a church bell: "Bob-by! Bob-by!" and it's both astute and endearing for him to have reduced our outsized love of a bench player to logic: "It's a blue collar city, and I'm a blue collar player." It's also not the whole quote. He started, "The city goes through a lot." He recognized pain in the present tense—it's happened and it's still happening—and a place can be a refuge simply by recognizing yourself in it. It had been for Bobby.

One of my old favorite restaurants, Smoke Shack, sucks now. I hate that I didn't get a chance to be right about it going downhill; no slow grief—just great and gone. Or maybe their pulled pork benedict with biscuits was never that good, or the memories brightened whenever I chewed some other slow-roasted pork. Maybe those are also more similar than not. With eight minutes left in the third, Jrue Holiday started up the floor in transition. He passed behind his back to a streaking Khris Middleton who gave it right back and Jrue leapt off one foot. Jae Crowder was skying in from nowhere for the block, but the ball didn't go up to the hoop—it went around Crowder's torso. Waiting there was Bobby Portis who took his time to grip the ball in two hands, bend, and slam it home.

"Bob-by! Bob-by!"

In the midst of pain, to do anything can be a triumph. And when I was about to leave and take stock of my heart there in the Milwaukee airport, I thought I recognized an empty cavity—some grief for the memory of a place that now only lived in my head—but I'd really left a bit of it in my brother's house. And empty space isn't all bad: it'd been used, I suppose, and growth can be a process of subtraction. I went back to Portland, yes, and all the way I thought of how much I love that my Milwaukee friends hugged me just as hard as the day I left no matter what our conversations were like, so powerful is memory. The friends I met in Portland hug pretty good too.

I also thought maybe when I loved Milwaukee most was when I missed it. It speaks in my coffee coasters, show posters, and brewery tee shirts, but that isn't something I can reciprocate. Leaving something alone is a way of loving it. It speaks for itself better than I can, if a place ever sits still enough to be spoken for at all.

Milwaukee woman to local WISN-12 journalist reporting live post-game outside Fiserv Forum:

"WE HAD SO MUCH FUN DOWN HERE

tonight. I can't—

Woman's friend screams into camera, runs off-screen

I can't even describe how much fun we had down here. It was like beautiful.

And everybody just enjoying themselves…

I'm borderline—I ain't gonna lie—I'm borderline drunk but everyone else is, so…

We're feeling good because we won because it's Bucks in Six!!!!!

We love you."

Giannis Antetokounmpo Postgame Media Availability:

Sam Amick: You're 26 years old. I've covered plenty of players who didn't seem like they figured the ego part out until their 30s. Who taught you about why that's important and to handle it that way?

Giannis: Usually, from my experience, when I think about like, *Oh, yeah, I did this, I'm so great, I had 30, I had 25-10-10*…Usually the next day you're going to suck, you know [smiles]? Simple as that. The next few days you're going to be terrible.

I figured out a mindset…when you focus on the past, that's your ego. *I did this. We were able to beat this team 4-0. I did this in the past. I won that in the past.* When I focus on the future, it's my pride. *Yeah, next game, Game*

5, I do this and this and this. I'm going to dominate. That's your pride talking. It doesn't happen.

You're right here. I kind of try to focus on the moment, in the present. That's humility. That's being humble... That's going out there, enjoying the game, competing at a high level. I think I've had people throughout my life that helped me with that. But that is a skill that I've tried to, like, kind of—how do you say, perfect it.

Amick: Master it?

Giannis: Yeah, master it. It's been working so far, so I'm not going to stop.

Valley Oop
(a Triptych)

"KNOCKED AWAY AND STOLEN BY HOLIDAY…"

Giannis should have bit on the fake, Devin Booker would say if he were honest—that it was supposed to be his night. The whole court slid right, and Devin Booker tugged the earth on a string. These moments are what make a prophecy, when you see the future unfurl in your head. When it's all imagined you can stretch out time itself like pasta dough. Malleable. It's before you have to explain anything, before you sign the lease, before you drive two-thousand miles yourself, before you congratulate yourself on being the best partner because you're giving so, so much, and she should love you for it. Before you convince your future employer this is the step your life is meant to take and convince yourself while you're at it. When there's a clear path, and that it is narrow is not a bug but a feature. Giannis was going to bite on the fake. It had been foretold. When all you have to say is: "yes."

"Phoenix has to foul…"

Khris Middleton had a suggestion. He's all the way behind the play, but just as Jrue thought it Khris pointed up. It is a silly thing to silently signal a teammate who cannot see you. Khris was praying. Every basketball sense said to pull the ball out and force a foul, but Jrue Holiday and Khris Middleton summoned a different sense. I still can't say if I believe in God, but I believe in surprise, and when I think about the ways God can still be real to me I'm not sure I mean much different than that. And Jrue threw it on high. Khris didn't will Jrue to pass—it is not proximity but rather movement that bonds a family together. Khris signaled his brother. Cause or coincidence, it happened.

"And Antetokounmpo throws it down!"

Eighteen thousand Phoenix fans counted to twelve for each of Giannis's free throws, and Giannis could have stared down any one or ten of them. He chose a TV camera. His mean mugs feature a prominent wrinkle in his nose—this was different. He could've shattered glass with his beady eyes and tense jaw. He looked into me and everyone thousands of miles back home or around the world. The arena didn't hush as much as ask itself if that just happened. Someone forgot to turn off DMX's "X Gon' Give It to Ya" from the previous possession. Giannis sent a message to the world, and the message was him.

Giannis had lived in Milwaukee for eight years by then, a year longer than I ever did. And the message wasn't meant for me specifically but I am once again trying to sneak on to the edges of a group photo. Giannis resisted the excitement of his teammates crowding him, and it was only when assistant coach Darvin Ham— who played for Milwaukee in 2001, the last time they were in the conference championship—approached that Giannis unleashed what he held back. Except he didn't raise his fists or scream. He jumped. And I don't need a seismometer to know the Deer District registered on the Richter scale. In Portland, a hundred fans in the bar jumped too. Fear shrunk me under my high top table. I did not share their excitement at first or seek to fit in with Milwaukee by imitation. I claimed the moment for myself. Euphoria can take away your breath and relax you at the same time. And I hunched there until something from the floor pushed upward, and the claiming took me toward the sky.

Gravity is a law and my people jumped and jumped again, for when we love we expend energy. Over and over they jumped, certain of an outcome coming back to Earth but pressing upward again anyway toward something, pressing on and on that someday we would take flight. That night, one of us did. And I know now that we love ourselves the most in the moment we can no longer crane our neck to the past. The once—just once—we can look down because the world's thinning tightrope turned flat and square miles wide. When the hoop looks like an ocean. When we love toward not just one future but any at all.

NBA Finals: Game 23, Win, 105-98
(Win; 4-2; 2021 NBA Champion: Milwaukee Bucks)

Ted Davis's Swan Song

"IT'S BEEN A FIFTY-YEAR JOURNEY!
Wisconsin! We've got a room on top of the world tonight!"

—TED DAVIS
Bucks radio announcer
on his last play-by-play call

106

A Letter

KAYLEE,

You are two years old now. In the rare times we are together, it is an avalanche of feeling to want to tell you anything I know about taking care of your self-esteem or buying a car or applying for a job, but none of it will stick and you're more interested in bubbles, so we do that instead. I'm guessing this is the first recorded thing you'll be sure I said to you.

When I was ten or eleven, I started feeling weird when your Papa told me how much he loved me. He didn't drop me off at school, roll down the window, and yell it for the whole senior class to hear, but it'd be in our car rides or as the years went on over the phone. I just didn't think I deserved it. What had I done for him anyway besides mow the lawn at semi-accurate angles? It confounded me for years, but what I know now is loving a child gives your parents something, and your grandparents something, and gives me something. I'm not sure I ever knew the definition of the word "coo" until I saw my own mother—your Mimi—around you. Time doesn't heal wounds, but sometimes you'll take a skin graft where you can get it. A baby can be a reset button. You were a chance for us to be the people we wished we could be. And so by loving you we get to love ourselves a way we never could. You're a second start from true zero where our first moments as uncle, aunt, parent, or grandparent are everything we've ever been in that identity.

Last month, I lived out of a hotel for a few weeks in Milwaukee and saw you many times. My desire to spoil you was also a desire to spoil myself. And it's no transaction—it's set in our bones through thousands of years of family and offspring across continents that here arrives a baby into our orbit and we give continuously and somehow receive in equal or greater measure. Matter can be neither created nor destroyed, but there is a making here. And so in the spirit of trying to give you something in this letter, I am also writing to give to myself.

I am writing to you (and myself) about orbits. Home is not a place that will always be the same and it is also never a single person. The way we tend to think about home is more of an area at a specific point in time when it's really a living organism, a thing you can choose to love for what it is and forgive it for who it isn't, or if you love it a whole lot, sometimes demand it tell itself the truth. And that place can be in orbit as close as Mercury or far like Pluto. Yet, as many orbits as we have around us, we orbit others as well. The moon orbits the earth—yes—but it orbits the sun too. And not a single one of earth's orbits of the sun is the same as the last. We're a little skinnier and elliptical in some years then a little wider and ovular in others, which means the moon counteracts in its own dance. Some orbits you count on will drift, but a drift won't burn out the sun—all of the galaxies and universes are in a delicate balance, spinning plate on top of spinning plate. And when Giannis Antetokounmpo talked like a man twice his age and said true humility is focusing on the present and that making small, good decisions stacks into success, I am asking you and also asking myself to think about who you allow in your orbit. Sometimes you'll distance yourself from someone or break orbits altogether, and sometimes you'll bring someone closer than you ever thought you would. This, I think, is when a person or a place or a thing becomes part of what we think of as our home. The 2021 Bucks were a team of seventeen players, a dozen or so coaches, and scores of staff whose orbits around each other aligned to produce a total eclipse. They caused a onetime shimmer like the northern lights that they could only achieve together. Each of those people are now part of each other's home. They will reunite in ten years, twenty, twenty-five. Their hairlines will recede. Some will pass away. But they made choices to be in each other's orbit, to bring one person closer when they dribbled over a screen, keep another just far enough away to throw an alley-oop, offer a hand to lift someone from the floor or distance to stew in a bad turnover, tightening and loosening all the time in the perfect way where on one hot July night they got to share the sugar cane splendor of being alive. More impressive than anything is the trust: that you might push away and be wrong then the second person will know to push themselves toward you again, or that you'll push a little and they'll know well enough to move further. We aren't much without the generosity, mutual kindness, and love of those we keep in our orbits. We wouldn't move at all.

I know now that while the Milwaukee I once called my own is gone, its people are worth keeping around. And I'd like to do a better job focusing on that instead of Friday Fish Fry or the Bronze Fonz. The 2021 Bucks helped keep me in your mother and Mimi and Papa's orbits. I shared this championship with them and other friends I wanted to stay in touch with even though I didn't have a clue how else I'd do that. The Bucks are one of the magnetic pulls between us and a way we hold onto each other as years pass. A text message analyzing a defense here, a funny gif there, pictures of our TV and snack set, or you in the Giannis onesie. That summer, I exited someone from my orbit entirely and pulled a little harder on someones I'd allowed to slacken. For a couple hours every other day watching these games I was home anywhere I could be found. I don't confess to know much, but ever since then I have been trying all the time to pay more attention to where people are in my orbit, and it's bore gift after gift. This includes your mother and father with whom I've always had a good relationship but had never said "I'm excited to see you" aloud until you were born. We've pulled in on each other.

What I'm saying is when you feel the pull toward independence, follow it. Just tend to those orbits in the spare moments of that all-important pursuit of your own life. When your mother weeps for you—and she will—hold her hand. When your father is trying to understand and you know he can't, hug him tight. These are small moments you may forget but they never will, and when you wonder what they expect from you for all that they've given you, know that every positive moment you've ever had with them is worth to them a lifetime of job promotions or getting the last open restaurant table. You can choose or choose not to pull on me, but mine is a door that will never close. I am here for you, for whenever I can help you, please know I can also help myself.

You are a salve for more than you know. Take it from me: I emptied space in my orbit that summer by pushing someone away, but I've found someone new who is showing me new terrains and oceans and forests of myself I'd never known. I may be wrong, but I may be right, and what I'm trying to hold on to even on days it feels impossible is choosing to be okay with being either because my people won't let me fall. And yours won't either.

With love,
Uncle Ben

Acknowledgments

THANK YOU TO THE ENTIRE TEAM AT Cornerstone Press who saw the vision for this book and embraced it, especially Brett Hill, Sophie McPherson, and Sam Bjork. Dr. Ross Tangedal couldn't have been a better publisher to work with from the first phone call through printing. So grateful to you all.

Thank you to artist Allen Parker II. You are proof the internet can occasionally be a great place.

Thank you to Bucks fans everywhere from Twitter to BlueSky to Discord to Fiserv and the Deer District. Special shoutout to Drew, Tim, and Matt Baumgartner. Our group chat started before the 2021 run and continues today. Shoutout as well to Ryan McCauley, Rob Moyer, and Ryan Jaeger.

Huge thanks to my writing mentors over the years who encouraged and nurtured me when I needed it: Joe Costa, Jim Kearney, Larry Watson, Tom Grimes, Debra Monroe, Doug Dorst, Karen Russell, Tim O'Brien, and many others who've guided me along the way.

Thank you to the faculty and my cohort at Texas State University's MFA program. Special thanks to Kaitlyn Burd, Taylor Kirby, Wade Dittburner, Jake Kemp, Will Pellett, and Brady Brickner-Wood. I love and appreciate you all.

Thank you to my friends Brendan Hilliard and Mark Yencheske who believed in me as a writer before I did.

Thank you to the following artists, without whom this book wouldn't have existed: The Hold Steady, Frightened Rabbit, Drive-by Truckers (and Jason Isbell), and MJ Lenderman. Different, but just as vital: Brian Eno.

Thank you to my Mom and my Dad to whom I owe so much. Thank you to my siblings, Bill, Brett, and Courtney. I'm inspired by each of you and am happy to have you as my family.

Thank you to my wife, Maire-Kate. It is my life's joy to be with you.

Ben McCormick was born in Wisconsin and now lives in Portland, Oregon. He earned an MFA at Texas State University, and his writing has appeared in places like *Ploughshares Blog*, *Harvard Review Online*, *The Pinch*, and *Passages North*. He's watched every Bucks game for the last seven seasons and is a lifelong fan.